# Uncharted, Unexplored, and Unexplained

## Scientific Advancements of the 19th Century

# Karl Benz

## and the
## Single Cylinder Engine

Mitchell Lane
PUBLISHERS

P.O. Box 196
Hockessin, Delaware
19707

# Uncharted, Unexplored, and Unexplained

## Scientific Advancements of the 19th Century

# Titles in the Series

**Visit us on the web: www.mitchelllane.com**
**Comments? email us: mitchelllane@mitchelllane.com**

# Uncharted, Unexplored, and Unexplained

## Scientific Advancements of the 19th Century

# Karl Benz

## and the
## Single Cylinder Engine

by John Bankston

# Uncharted, Unexplored, and Unexplained

JB
Benz B

*Mitchell Lane*
**PUBLISHERS**

Printing      1    2    3    4    5    6    7    8
     Library of Congress Cataloging-in-Publication Data
Bankston, John, 1974-
          Karl Benz and the single cylinder engine / John Bankston
               p. cm. — (Uncharted, unexplored, and unexplained, scientific advancements of the 19th century)
     Includes bibliographical references (p.) and index.
          ISBN 1-58415-244-3 (lib bdg.)
     1. Benz, Karl, 1844 - 1929 —Juvenile literature. 2. Automobile engineers—Germany—Biography—Juvenile literature. [1. Benz, Karl. 1844-1929. 2. Automobile engineers. 3. Engineers. 4. Inventors.] I. Title. II. Series. Uncharted, unexplored and unexplained.
     TL140.B4 B35 2004
     629.222'092—dc22

                                                                      2003024049

**ABOUT THE AUTHOR:** Born in Boston, Massachusetts, John Bankston has written over three dozen biographies for young adults profiling scientists like Jonas Salk and Alexander Fleming, celebrities like Mandy Moore and Alicia Keys, great achievers like Alfred Nobel, and master musicians like Mozart. He worked in Los Angeles, California as a producer, screenwriter and actor. Currrently he is in preproduction on *Dancing at the Edge*, a semi-autobiographical film he hopes to film in Portland, Oregon. Last year he completed his first young adult novel, *18 to Look Younger.*

**PHOTO CREDITS:** Cover: Hulton/Archive; pp. 6, 9, 17, 20 Hulton/Archive; pp. 12, 23 Daimler-Benz; p. 26 Science Photo Library; pp. 28, 30 Daimler-Benz; pp. 33, 36 Hulton/Archive; p.39 Gotschke, Walter.

**PUBLISHER'S NOTE:** This story is based on the author's extensive research, which he believes to be accurate. Documentation of such research is contained on page 47.

The internet sites referenced herein were active as of the publication date. Due to the fleeting nature of some web sites, we cannot guarantee they will all be active when you are reading this book.

# Scientific Advancements of the 19th Century

# Karl Benz

## and the Single Cylinder Engine

*For Your Information

Karl Benz designed the electric ignition and water-cooled engine that are still used in automobiles today.

# 1

# Tired of Biking

As he struggled to ride his bike, Karl Benz grew frustrated. The streets of Mannheim, Germany were better suited for a horse and carriage than for bicycling. Muddy and hilly, the road near his home made even a short trip on a bike completely exhausting. The bike he rode was pretty funny looking, with its tall front tire and stumpy rear one. It also wasn't very practical. Built for fun, the bike was a poor substitute for a horse and carriage. Pedaling long distances was nearly impossible. When it rained, the rider got soaked. Leaning his body into the pedals and maneuvering his bike around ruts and potholes, Karl just knew there had to be a better way to get around.

It wasn't the first time he'd thought about the problem. But that day he went into his workshop and began to build something that would be much better than either a bike or a horse.

In the 1870s, inventors like Karl were developing "horseless carriages." These were vehicles that were powered by an engine instead of a beast. But Karl didn't just want to imitate others. He wanted to create a brand new vehicle. The vehicle he imagined would be perfect for the dawning twentieth century. He felt confident that one day it could replace horses and carriages altogether.

Karl planned to power it with an engine that he had designed. His work occurred at a time everyone seemed to be in an invention race. From locomotives to telegraphs, the way people lived changed so radically, that the 1800s were considered revolutionary.

In fact, beginning early in the nineteenth century, the era had a name: "The Industrial Revolution." Our modern era is rooted in this time period. Most of the products we use today are mass-produced, from cars to computers. This use of mass-produced products began during the Industrial Revolution. Before that time, most things in common usage were handmade by skilled craftsmen. Afterward, many of these same items were made in factories as machines pumped out thousands of identical products.

Karl Benz dreamed of a vehicle that combined the best of both worlds: the relatively low cost of mass production with the elegant attention to detail that is found in handmade products.

He came along at the right time. During the 1800s, in the United States and in countries across Europe, people moved from farm-based economic systems to manufacturing systems. In 1800, almost half of Britain's workers were employed in farms. By 1900 less than 10 percent made their living this way. This revolution was driven by machines, not weapons. Machines ran railroad locomotives and factory equipment. And these machines were driven by steam.

Invented in 1705 by Thomas Newcomen and improved by James Watt sixty-four years later, the steam engine ran on a simple principle. Fuel (mainly wood or coal) was burned under a boiler that was filled with water. Soon the water would turn into steam. Then the steam was released to power the machinery. For over a century, steam was employed to run everything from stagecoaches to tractors.

Unfortunately, early steam engines were very unpredictable and dangerous. Think about what would happen if the spout of a teakettle is plugged up while water continues to boil inside. With nowhere to go,

8

A color print of a steam-powered locomotive train. Steam engines helped fuel the Industrial Revolution which made the automobile possible.

the pressure inside the teakettle becomes enormous. At a certain point, it is likely to explode.

Steam engines had the same problem. Many people who worked with them were severely burned or even killed when they blew up.

Steam engines weren't just terribly dangerous. In many cases, they were also terribly inefficient. The boiler required to power a smaller vehicle such as a car was too large to be practical. Despite this obstacle, experiments to construct a steam powered car continued until well into the 1890s.

In Europe and in North America, many inventors who were working on automobiles hoped to replace steam with something that would be both safer *and* more practical. Many thought the answer lay with the internal combustion engine. The construction of this engine was complicated, and many people contributed to its development. Yet one man combined the inventions of others with his own designs, constructing a car that was a practical alternative to both horses and bicycles. In the process, he developed systems like the electric ignition and the water-cooled engine that are still used today.

Karl Benz didn't plan on starting his own automotive revolution. Raised in poverty by a single mother, he eventually owned one of the first successful car companies in the world. His company is still in existence more than a century later. As he developed his car, he benefited both from his wife's never-ending encouragement and promotions of his efforts and from the existence of a major competitor just down the road.

The story of Karl Benz is not just a story about the internal combustion engine but also about the car it powered. Its development changed millions of lives.

# Cugnot

*Wars are horrible. In every war lives are lost, and the costs in terms of money and human suffering are enormous. Yet even in the most tragic of circumstances, benefits arise. Inventions created to help fight wars often end up helping people in times of peace.*

*New or improved vehicles have often come from the battlefield. Airplanes became more reliable following World War I, World War II brought the Jeep into existence, and today the Hummer is a popular consumer vehicle after being battle-tested in several "hot spots" around the globe.*

*One of the first "car designers" was a French army engineer named Nicolas-Joseph Cugnot. Born in 1725, he invented a new type of rifle in his early years as a soldier. After serving during the Seven Years War against Great Britain, he went home to Paris in 1763. He began working on a steam-operated carriage a few years later. In 1769, he got it to run.*

*Considered by many to be the first self-propelled vehicle, it consisted of a wooden frame and three large iron-rimmed wheels with thick wooden spokes. A boiler holding 400 gallons of water and the steam engine were suspended over the front of the vehicle. It was designed to carry a cannon or other heavy equipment. Because it weighed several tons, it could only move about two or three miles per hour. Even then, it required too much water for such a small load to be practical. Every fifteen minutes it had to stop and allow the steam power to build up.*

*Besides inventing what some consider the first car, Cugnot also experienced the first car crash. In one of his demonstrations, his vehicle hit a garden wall. Despite this setback, Cugnot continued to work on a variety of steam-powered vehicles. None of them proved very practical for regular use in war or in peace.*

This photograph of Karl Benz was taken when he was a student at Karlsruhe Polytechnikum.

# 2

# Sailing with Karl

Before railroads sliced across the United States, journeys to the west took weeks, even months. Travelers risked everything from harsh weather to deadly attacks from native Indian tribes. Starting in the 1840s, that began to change. People were protected inside the passenger cars of railroad trains. Within a couple of decades, trips to places like California could be made in a matter of days. The dramatic population growth of the western U.S. can be traced to development of the railroad.

In Europe, the railroad's impact was similar, although somewhat less dramatic. In Germany, the first railway line opened in 1835 between Nuremberg and Furth. Within a few years, railroad tracks cut through many other parts of the country. It was a period of enormous unrest in the region. The tracks connected a country that was beginning to pull apart.

They also helped connect the outside world to Karlsruhe, a town in southwest Germany near the French border in the state of Baden-Wurttemberg. It was here that Karl Friedrich Benz (sometimes written as Carl) was born on November 25, 1844.

The impact of the railroad on Karl's life didn't take long to become very personal. His father, Johann, had a job working as an engineer on a train. Unfortunately, when Karl was only two his father was severely injured in an accident at work. Soon after the accident, Johann died of pneumonia. As a widow, Karl's mother Josephine received a small railroad pension. The money was hardly enough to support a family, even one that consisted of only two people.

To save money, Josephine sold their house and moved in with her family. She took a job as a cook and did sewing for extra income. Even then, there was barely enough money.

So, from a very young age, Karl worked. Instead of doing the type of manual labor jobs that were common during that era, he used his mind to earn money. Very early in his life, he had shown that he had a great deal of mechanical ability. He could take apart a piece of machinery and put it back together again. Afterwards it usually ran better than it had before. His special talent was fixing watches. Even when he could barely read, he was able to get a stopped timepiece to start running again. Soon everyone seemed to know about the Benz boy and his talent for repairing watches.

Karl's mother encouraged his interest in the latest technologies, and in the 1850s photography was a relatively recent development. Although it was expensive and cumbersome, the process of taking pictures attracted professionals and hobbyists. Many early photographers visited the Black Forest near his home. Earning its name for the very dark, almost black pine trees that lay within, the Black Forest was a major tourist attraction. Whenever he could, Karl asked the photographers questions about their equipment. He was fascinated by the science of it all. Just as important, it didn't take him long to find a new way to make money.

In the 1850s, there was no such thing as a "One Hour Photo." Since many of the out-of-towners wanted to see their pictures quickly, Karl built a darkroom in his mother's house and learned to handle the dangerous chemicals needed to develop pictures. Between watches and photographs, Karl was able to make enough money to help out his mother.

He did more than just work. His father's work on the railroad must have made a deep impression on the boy. He enjoyed drawing pictures of steam locomotives, complete with smoke curling out of the stack.

Despite the family's meager circumstances, Karl's mother tried to ensure that her son was well educated. By the age of eight, he was attending the Karlsruhe Grammar School. As a teenager he attended a lyceum, or private high school. The tuition was difficult for Josephine to pay—it was almost 20 percent of her pension. Still, she believed it was worth it. The school emphasized the sciences, a subject that Karl loved. His mother even managed to buy her son some crude lab equipment and he soon constructed a rudimentary laboratory in the attic.

At the age of eighteen he enrolled at Karlsruhe's Polytechnic, also called the "Fridericiana." It was probably the oldest technical college in Germany, and it enjoyed a good reputation across the country.

At the Polytechnic Karl studied everything from mechanical engineering to drafting, learning to draw complicated plans for machines. He even worked for a time as an assistant to a physics professor. Still, one professor's comments stayed with Karl long after he left the Polytechnic. Ferdinand Redtenbacher said the steam engine was incredibly impractical and someday would have to be replaced. Karl began to wonder what would replace it.

One of the alternatives was something his teacher called an "explosion engine." Powered by gas instead of steam, the first successful version was designed by Jean Etienne Lenoir, who used the gas given off by burning coal.

The year after its invention in 1860, Karl traveled to a factory in Stuttgart. The Max Eyth Machine Tool Factory had recently installed one of Lenoir's gas engines. Karl watched it, fascinated, thinking about it the way he thought about watches: *How could he take it apart? How could he make it run better?*

Then again, maybe Karl would just have to develop a better engine.

In 1864, Karl graduated with an engineering degree. He also drifted. In less than six years he worked for several companies. Because his mother was very ill, he initially took a job with a local locksmith so he could care for her. After she recovered, he worked as a draftsman and as a designer. He managed a small business and was briefly employed by a company on the nearby French border that manufactured locomotives. In every instance, Karl quit or was fired because he couldn't focus. He tried to concentrate on the work at hand, but he always returned to his dream of building a better engine.

The many jobs he held actually served a purpose. When he was working for an engine manufacturer, he began to think about building a horseless carriage. By working with engines he learned how to power one. He briefly worked at a wagon and pump company in Mannheim, about twenty-five miles north of Karlsruhe. Because of the job, he found a town he was ready to settle down in.

Karl didn't want to build what others told him to build. He didn't want to follow other people's plans. Mostly these plans did nothing more than slightly improve existing machines. He wanted to do more. The only way he could do that was by striking out on his own. Karl had to work for himself.

In 1870, Karl's mother died. Losing the person who had supported him and believed in his ambitions was devastating. But it also might have inspired him to realize that life was short and that dreams are worth pursuing.

By the following year, Germany was celebrating its victory over France in the Franco-Prussian War. As sometimes happens when a war is over, jobs were hard to find. In addition, Karl had met a young woman named Bertha Ringer. He wanted to get married. So he made a courageous move. If he couldn't find a job working for someone else, he'd work for himself. He gambled when he began the "Iron Foundry and Machine Shop" with a partner named August Ritter. Inside the shop, Karl spent every free moment imagining new vehicles and the engines that would run them. In between filling the orders of his customers, he began to construct alternatives to the steam engine.

Unfortunately, Karl's head was in the clouds when it should have been in the business. The Iron Foundry was failing. Worse, the deal he had signed with Ritter gave his partner sole possession of the entire company if it lost too much money. Karl realized he could be back trying to find a job less than a year after going out on his own.

Karl Benz (in light suit) on a trip with his family with one of his first cars, which was built in 1893 and powered by a single cylinder 3 h.p. engine. His friend Theodor Leibig is in the car on the right.

Salvation arrived from an unexpected source.

Bertha Ringer had grown up in Pforzheim and was in her early twenties when she met the young inventor. Bertha realized that Karl was having problems. She asked if there was anything she could do.

There was.

Karl needed a loan, desperately. Turning to the woman he loved to bail him out was an unconventional choice. But then Karl was never a conventional man.

Bertha had a dowry, a sum of money given to a young woman by her family at the time of her wedding. There was just one problem. Karl and Bertha weren't married yet. To Bertha, that fact—like Karl's financial problems—was just a tiny obstacle to be overcome. She got access to her dowry and gave it to him lock, stock and barrel. The cash was enough for him to buy out Ritter's interest. Now he was his own man. [1]

"In those days when our little boat of life threatened to capsize," Karl later wrote in his autobiography, "only one person stood steadfastly by me: My wife. She bravely set new sails of hope." [2]

After their marriage on July 20, 1872, Bertha would have many opportunities to keep the ship of Benz from sinking.

The eighteenth century revolutions in the United States and France inspired a wave of similar revolts across much of Europe during the following century. In 1848, a series of revolutions swept across the independent states of Germany. The goals of the revolutionaries were fairly simple.

They wanted to see these states united and combined with parts of modern-day Austria, Hungary, and Poland. Rights should be granted to the citizens, such as the right to vote, the right of freedom of the press, religion, and assembly along with numerous other rights familiar to people living in the United States today.

King Frederick William IV of Prussia

Armed uprisings early in 1848 in Vienna, Berlin, and other areas produced some initial successes. The rulers of many of the states were frightened enough to give in to the revolutionaries' demands. A National Assembly was convened in the city of Frankfurt in May, 1848. It had two main problems. One was that its members had such serious political divisions that it was hard to agree on anything. The other was that it didn't truly represent the people. It was sarcastically nicknamed the "professor's parliament" because most of its members were civil servants and university professors who were idealistic rather than practical.

As a result, the assembly made little progress, though it drew up what was termed "Basic Rights for the German People." It also offered the position of Emperor to the Prussian King Frederick William IV early in 1849. He not only turned it down but also criticized the states that had already approved of the idea. Many of the members of the Assembly went home. Soldiers soon disbanded what was left of the Assembly. Many of the former revolutionaries were captured. Some were executed. The revolution was over. By 1851, even the Basic Rights had been abolished.

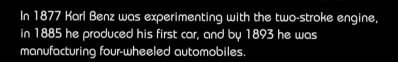

In 1877 Karl Benz was experimenting with the two-stroke engine, in 1885 he produced his first car, and by 1893 he was manufacturing four-wheeled automobiles.

# 3

# Engine-Ering

Maybe Karl Benz's young bride Bertha helped him to focus. Maybe he was just worried about losing all the money she'd given him. Whatever the cause, Karl had to pay close attention to his business. It was not an overnight success. Economic conditions in Germany still weren't ideal.

During his occasional idle moments, he recalled the challenge that his Polytechnic professor Ferdinand Redtenbacher had given him: using machine power instead of muscle power or steam power to move people. His struggles as he rode his bicycle made the challenge more personal.

Steam engines were already becoming obsolete. Karl's professor had wondered what would replace them. The answer arrived with the 1870's. The internal combustion engine controlled explosive power by keeping it inside the machinery. It was an entirely different concept from the steam engine. In a steam engine, the fuel is burned in a space that is separate from the engine. In an internal combustion engine the fuel is burned (combusted) inside the motor.

Experiments with such an engine had begun over seventy years earlier when Switzerland's François Isaac de Rivaz used hydrogen and oxygen for fuel. His "car" didn't run very well, nor did the vehicles invented by Samuel Brown and Jean Étienne Lenoir. Alphonse de Rochas got a patent in 1862 for a four-stroke engine—which means no one could copy his design without paying for it. But de Rochas never built it.

Still, even in failure the research of all these men guided the efforts of Eugen Langen and Nicolaus August Otto. Located less than fifty miles from Mannheim, the pair began working on an engine of their own. It was impossible for Karl not to hear rumors of their work, and of their progress.

In 1876, Otto perfected the internal combustion engine when he invented the four-stroke motor. The power comes from a piston that is placed tightly inside a cylinder and moves up and down. A connecting rod links the piston to a crankshaft, which converts the up and down movements to a circular motion that turns the wheels of the car through a series of gears and shafts.

The four-stroke sequence starts with what is called the intake stroke. The piston moves down in the cylinder, while a valve at the top opens to admit a mixture of fuel and air into the cylinder.

The second stroke is called the compression stroke. The piston moves up. That has the effect of compressing the fuel and air mixture. When the piston nearly reaches the top of the cylinder and the compression is at its greatest, an ignition system produces an electrical spark.

That ignites the fuel and air mixture, which creates enough energy to push the piston back down. This is called the power stroke.

When the piston reaches the bottom of its stroke, another valve at the top of the cylinder opens. The piston moves back up and pushes the exhaust gases out of the cylinder through the open valve. This is the exhaust stroke.

When the piston reaches the top of the cylinder, it is ready to begin the sequence again.

Although many different fuels were tested in running the motor—kerosene, oil, anything else that was flammable—it turned out gasoline

An early catalog for the Benz engine. The world's first successful two-stroke engine had been patented by Scotsman Dugald Clerk in 1878. Benz improved upon it in his fuel and air pump design, which eliminated the hazard of the fuel mixture igniting inside the pump.

was the best because it burned so easily. Ironically, gasoline began as a useless by-product of the oil refining process. Oil was used in lamps and for lubricating, but in the beginning gasoline was discarded.

Karl had a growing family to support following the birth of his sons Eugen in 1873 and Richard the next year (eventually the Benzes would have three more children). He was convinced that developing a vehicle and the engine to power it would meet his family's financial needs. Starting in 1878, he focused on building gas engines. Since Otto had a patent on a four-stroke engine, no one could manufacture or sell the design without his permission. So Karl focused on a two-stroke engine. It has a compression stroke (when the piston moves up) and a power stroke (when the piston moves down).

Since a two-stroke engine produces power for every turn of the crankshaft (as opposed to every *other* turn in a four-stroke) it is more powerful than the same sized four-stroke engine. Today two-stroke engines power small machines such as lawnmowers, leaf blowers, chainsaws, dirt bikes, and snowmobiles.

Developing his engine wasn't an easy process for Karl. As author W. Robert Nitske says, "In the exacting work of engine development, there were no windfalls, no accidental stumblings on solutions of difficult problems. Every action was painstakingly planned, minutely diagrammed, carefully executed and hopefully tested; and the tedious, detailed work went on for year after year." [1]

So Karl persevered. In 1880, he celebrated the New Year with a great leap forward. His first successful two-stroke, one-horsepower engine sputtered, then began running smoothly. He was ready for the next step, building a vehicle.

He soon convinced photographer Emil Buhler and several other men to invest in "The Mannheim Gas Engine Manufacturing Company." The new business made the most of Karl's talents, allowing him to focus on the latest technology in engines. Unfortunately his investors didn't share Karl's dream. They wanted profits, and quickly. Karl walked away.

It didn't take long for him to find men who were willing to invest in another company. This one would both build engines and a car to put them in. So long as Karl focused most of his time on moneymaking activities, his new investors were willing to let him construct a "horseless carriage" as well.

In October of 1883, Karl began working at the company that bore his name: Benz & Co. Rheinische Gasmotoren-Fabrik. His primary investors were Max Rose and Friedrich Esslinger. They owned a shop in Mannheim that sold many different items. Some of these items were bicycles, which is probably how Karl met them. They may have shared his frustrations at its limitations.

It didn't take long for their faith to be rewarded. The company soon expanded to include a workforce of more than two dozen men. Karl finally had enough money so that he could concentrate on working on his car.

The two-stroke engine was a great design, but it had several disadvantages. The main one was that even though it generated a lot of power for its size, it tended to wear out quickly if it was used constantly. Much later, people would also discover that it polluted the air much more than four-stroke engines. Karl needed a bigger, more durable engine to power the vehicle of his imagination. Then he learned that the patent on the four-stroke engine that Otto designed had run out. It was perfect timing!

For two years, Karl worked on his design. In some ways his first vehicle looked more like a tricycle than a car. It had two large rear wheels and a single smaller wheel in front. That made it easier for Karl to steer it.

His first vehicle showed off many features familiar to modern car buyers. A pinion—a small cogwheel that meshed with a larger cogwheel or a rack—was connected to the steering wheel. On the other end, it was connected to a rack that controlled the wheels. It had an electrical ignition system connected to a battery, rear springs and a water-cooled engine. The engine ran on benzene, a petroleum-based product that was very similar to gasoline. Back then benzene could only be found at drugstores—there were no gas stations of course.

The first public demonstration came in the fall of 1885, just two years after the company's birth. Karl and Bertha climbed proudly into the car, as a group of reporters and onlookers eagerly watched. Unfortunately all the excitement must have affected Karl's concentration. He forgot to steer!

As a result, the first public demonstration of the car also produced what may have been Germany's first car crash. Fortunately, Karl running his new vehicle into a brick wall didn't affect its reviews. Newspapers reported on the car, and even as he improved its design the vehicle began to win awards.

Karl Benz received German patent #37435 for his design of "Patent-Motorwagen-Benz" on January 29, 1886. Many people consider that document to be the "birth certificate" of the modern automobile.

1st page of the patent awarded to Karl Benz in 1886 for his car design, showing a picture of the vehicle. This gas-powered motor tricycle was one of the first automobiles.

Unlike most births, however, there wasn't much of a celebration.

As author Nitske says, "Benz, like most of the daring pioneers before and after him, received ridicule and abuse. Many people pitied the apparently sane man who had spent considerable effort and a lot of money on an entirely useless, sputtering and smoking horseless carriage. Some astute observers pointed out that, as long as there were enough horses in the country, it was ridiculous to buy a motor vehicle."[2]

People seemed to take this advice to heart. Hardly anyone was buying Karl's new invention. The main problem was that Karl's car, and ones like it, were considered "rich men's toys." They weren't as reliable as a horse and broke down more often than a bicycle. There were other obstacles. Many areas didn't allow motor vehicles on their roads. In London, a law dating back to 1865 required all self-propelled vehicles such as steam cars and automobiles to have a man walking ahead of them holding a red flag. The signal was to let those with horses know that a car was coming. The speed limit was four miles per hour. That law kept cars off London streets for three decades.

Karl needed to prove that his vehicle was more than just a toy—it was a practical means of transportation, more comfortable than a bicycle, faster than a horse and carriage. Once again, his wife would make all the difference.

Many improvements made to bicycles in the 1800s were later adopted by early car manufacturers. Of course, bikes weren't powered by engines, but by "people power." In fact, the first bike–called a hobby horse–didn't even have pedals. It was developed by Baron von Drais in 1817 in Paris. The seat was low enough for riders to push it with their feet. With its wooden wheels, it wasn't practical for anything outside of a park or off a garden path.

Pedals came along nearly fifty years later when the velocipede (a French word that means "fast feet") was introduced. It had a large front wheel and smaller rear wheel. Made of wood, it was also known as the "boneshaker" because it gave a rough ride over cobblestone roads.

It was replaced by a metal model in 1870. Rubber tires and wheels with spokes gave a much smoother ride. The pedals were fixed to the huge front wheel, and the bigger the wheel the faster it would go. It was the first time that the term bicycle ("two wheels") was used to describe the vehicle and its popularity took off. Unfortunately, if the rider hit a ditch or an obstacle he'd go right over the handlebars and "take a header."

For women in skirts and gentlemen too dignified to ride such a contraption, the tricycle was a reasonable alternative. It was here that such devices as rack and pinion steering, later used by Karl Benz, were first developed.

It took air-filled tires, chains and wheels of the same size to produce a bike that today's riders would recognize. Introduced in the 1890s, this version provided a practical alternative to horses, and it was cheaper and more reliable than cars. In the 1870s, bikes cost more than most people made in six months. Twenty years later, they cost a fraction as much and were much better made.

Bertha Benz was a never-ending-source of encouragement and support to her husband Karl Benz.

# 4

# Bertha's Caper

"We are going to visit Grandma," the note read. It was early one August morning in 1888 when Bertha Benz wrote this message, gathered her two sons, and left their house in Mannheim. Karl was still sleeping. [1]

The inventor was probably surprised to wake up to a nearly empty house. He soon realized that his wife had left with fifteen-year-old Eugen and fourteen-year-old Richard in tow. He would have been even more startled if he'd realized what she was up to.

Bertha Benz wasn't "visiting Grandma." She was on a mission to save her husband's company. She planned to take the car to do it.

Already she'd done everything she could to keep his dream alive. She'd found customers for his engine business, and motivated him to keep working on his car. But Karl always seemed to be plagued by doubts. He continually worried that the car wasn't good enough to sell to the public, even though he kept improving it in the three years since his first demonstration. Every time he was certain the change he'd made would be the last. Yet with every improvement, all he saw were new problems.

29

Bertha realized her husband's delays could wreck the company. He needed to begin selling cars to the public. The only way he could do that was if the public wanted to buy them. But the people who could afford to buy Karl's car had doubts about how reliable it was. Others didn't understand how it was propelled. The workings of the internal combustion were a mystery to them. Some even thought that it was the work of the devil. Whatever the reasons, people just weren't lining up to purchase it. This lack of success caused Karl to doubt himself. So Bertha took it upon herself to conduct a practical test that would prove how safe and reliable the vehicle was.

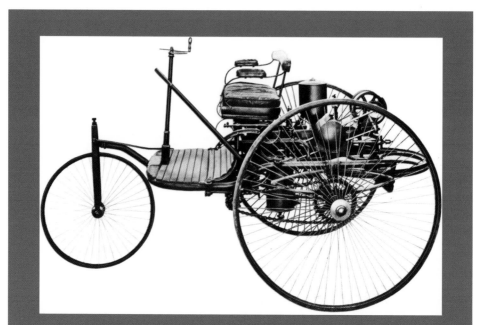

The first automobile built by Karl Benz reached a speed of eight miles per hour. The tubular frame and wire spoke wheels resembeled those of a bicycle.

At that time, women who were married to business owners didn't even operate their own horse and carriages, let alone try to drive motor vehicles. Bertha figured if a woman could drive the car with her children without her husband coming along, then men would be much more likely to buy it.

So, on that clear summer morning, she snuck out of the house. With the help of her two sons, she pushed the vehicle from the workshop onto the road. When they were far enough away that the sound of its engine wouldn't disturb her sleeping husband, she started the car. [2]

The three Benzes embarked on a sixty-five mile road trip. It would take them over unpaved roads from Mannheim to Pforzheim. They'd cross through part of the Black Forest. There would be no service stations, no telephones, no tow trucks along the route they chose. They were on their own.

In the late 1800s, it was an incredible journey.

Though the car was underpowered, it went along without many problems during the flat stretches. When they came to a hill, the boys had to hop off and push. The water-cooled engine needed constant replenishment. Bertha paused the car long enough to scoop water from puddles alongside the road numerous times during the trip. In the towns they passed through, she used public wells. The frequent stopping and starting wore down the brakes. In one town they had to hire a shoemaker to put strips of leather over the brakes. Once the chains broke, and they had to go to a blacksmith to get those repaired.

The shoemakers and blacksmiths were rooted in another era, an era Benz's invention would soon almost completely erase.

The toughest problem was fuel. Benzene wasn't a common product. People used this very flammable liquid to get stains from their clothes, which wasn't the safest idea. The best place to buy it was from a pharmacy, but it came in such small bottles that Bertha wound up buying out one druggist's entire stock.

The sun was setting as they approached the end of their trip. The car just couldn't make it up one final hill. A curious farmer gave them a hand, then Bertha and her sons coasted into Pforzheim.

She headed for the telegraph office to let her anxious husband know that she and the two boys were not only safe but also completely successful. They had made history's first long road trip.

Bertha's bravery made Karl's car known throughout Europe. The story about how she took off on the first road trip became instantly famous. Today it is as well known in Germany as legends about Abraham Lincoln growing up in a log cabin are in the United States. Bertha Benz had a good head for publicity. Unfortunately, her adventure didn't translate into sales.

Nor did the trip that she inspired. Soon after Bertha's return, Karl drove 200 miles to Munich to show off his car at a trade fair. He received a gold medal. But he only attracted one customer—who was committed to a mental hospital before Karl could deliver a car to him.

The problem—there were still very few people who wanted to actually buy one—even the lucky few who could afford such an expensive "toy." It was Karl's engine and the car's relative durability that attracted interest, but its odd three-wheeled design turned off many potential buyers.

Karl seemed to suddenly be opposing progress; only a few years before he was the one innovating. To him a three-wheeled car made sense. It was light, it was easy to steer. It was different. Unfortunately, to his investors, his potential customers, even his wife, it just wasn't practical. Four-wheeled vehicles had been around as long as horses pulled carts, and one with three wheels just didn't make sense.

By now Karl was not the only one making decisions. Before he'd stood alone, watching every step of the production process. But despite the lack of orders for his cars, the company was rapidly expanding. The gas engine business was thriving. In 1890, Karl's company became

Germany's second-largest engine manufacturing company. Two new partners came into the business and assumed important roles. Friedrich von Fischer would work in administration, while Julius Ganns would work in sales. Karl would focus on engineering.

They urged him to improve the car. Besides changing the design to four wheels, they wanted him to move to a two-cylinder engine that would increase its speed.

Pioneer motorist and aviator Frank Hedges Butler driving his Benz car. He was one of the first people in England to own an automobile.

At first Karl resisted altering the product he'd built from scratch, but eventually he gave in. In 1893, Karl began producing a four-wheeled vehicle, which he called the Victoria. Karl gave the car its name to celebrate his victory over the challenge of designing a steering system for a four-wheeled car. Despite all the improvements that he had made, sales remained slow.

Introduced in 1894, the Velo was designed with a more compact shape and a better engine. As its name reflected—Velo is the Latin word for "swift"—it also drove faster. It reached a speed of twelve miles per hour. In spite of the improvements, it sold for less than 500 dollars.

It was the first large-scale production car, with more than a thousand being sold in its first five years.

By 1897 Karl's company was building cars with more than one cylinder. One was the Phaeton, which accommodated four passengers in comfort. The Ideal was introduced in 1898 and seemed "ideal" for conversation. It also held four passengers, with the Ideal's driver sitting in what we would think of as the rear seat. A lower front seat faced the driver and allowed the passengers to look up at him, or watch the scenery. It was kind of like sitting backwards in the passenger car of a train. Although this setup was probably not the safest method for driving, it certainly made the Ideal one of history's most unusual automobiles.

In 1899, Karl's new Tonneau produced nine horsepower and had a speed of thirty miles an hour. He sounded a note of caution—maybe it was time to build better roads before increasing how fast cars could go.

He also showed a certain amount of stubbornness. He continued to drive the three-wheeled motorized vehicle he invented, leaving his four-wheeled innovations to his customers.

As the new century began, Karl Benz's company had sold nearly 3,000 cars. Though that figure seems very low to us today, at that time his company was the largest automotive manufacturer in the world, with more than 400 employees. But it was not the only one. Any business that earns a profit faces competition sooner or later. Karl's competition would come sooner, and it would come largely from two men. One of them, the inventor of the first motorcycle, lived just sixty miles away. The other man was several thousand miles away, in Detroit, Michigan. He was building his own car in a small shed. His name was Henry Ford.

# History

After World War I, the majority of Germans suffered as their country struggled to pay the harsh war debts imposed on them by the victorious Allies. Many people lost their jobs and prices rose dramatically. In this environment, Adolf Hitler gained popular support by promising a return to German pride and honor. Instead, he would eventually lead his country into the horrors of World War II.

Hitler called Karl Benz and Gottlieb Daimler "among the great pioneers of humanity in the sphere of transport"[3] and his first car was a top of the line Mercedes. After walking away from an accident in which the other car was demolished, he vowed that he would never drive any other brand. Although he disliked driving, Hitler showed his admiration for Benz's cars by always being driven in a Mercedes.

The company Karl began also contributed to the war effort, though he had died by that time. During World War II, Daimler-Benz was one of more than 1,000 German companies that employed "guest workers" from concentration camps. Mercedes-Benzes was the most common choice of the German Army for staff cars. The company provided the engines for fighter planes and ships. They built tanks and torpedo warheads. After the war, the Marshall Plan rebuilt a devastated Germany and ensured the company's survival. Daimler-Benz benefited from the support of the Allies as the company went back to doing what it did best, building cars.

Besides, Daimler-Benz was hardly alone in its support for Hitler's war effort. Volkswagen got its start because Hitler believed his countrymen should all own inexpensive, reliable cars. BMW supplied the military. Even the United State's General Motors Opel division supported Germany in the early years of Hitler's rule.

German engineer and inventor Gottlieb Daimler (1834-1900) built the world's first motorcycle.

# 5

# Race Cars

The car business has always been a competitive one. Even in the 1890s, better-designed cars quickly replaced earlier models. As Karl Benz's company grew more successful, competition began nipping at his heels.

Gottlieb Daimler lived in Canstatt, a town near Stuttgart. That was less than sixty miles from Karl. He'd patented an internal combustion engine five months before Karl gave a public display of his own design. Still, Karl is credited with being the true inventor of the car. Daimler's innovation was slapped onto the frame of a bicycle, which created the world's first motorcycle.

Daimler wasn't as interested in cars as he was in engines. After testing the first motorcycle in 1885, he attached a larger, one-cylinder engine to a horse carriage the next year. He also built engines for everything from boats to streetcars.

By 1890, Daimler was starting to give Karl a run for his money. That same year, the French automotive industry got its start when Rene Panhard and Emile Levassor bought the rights to produce cars with Daimler's engine. Five years later, one of their cars won a race from Paris to Bordeaux against seventeen competitors.

Karl hated speed. He braked for horses, and wondered why he should ever produce a car that went faster than twenty miles per hour. He especially hated auto racing with its noise and danger. No matter how hard his partners tried to convince him, he refused to enter a Benz car in a race. But nothing earned a car company more customers than a winner at a race.

The Daimler company was much more aggressive than Benz's about getting people to buy their cars. Daimler was a much better businessman than Karl. When an Austrian businessman and diplomat named Emil Jellinik offered to set up a dealership and buy several dozen cars, he had one condition. He wanted the cars to be named after his daughter. Because of Emil Jellinik's request, one of the most prestigious names in automobiles was born. The little girl's name was Mercedes.

The car made its debut in 1901. It had many new features, including a powerful yet lightweight engine and a low center of gravity. Even today, it looks somewhat like a modern sports car. But within a few yards after starting up in front of a large crowd, it broke down.

The setback was only temporary. At the Nice Automobile Week not long afterward, it created a sensation. Its speed, its power and its workmanship impressed everyone.

"We have entered the Mercedes era!" [1] wrote an important French journalist.

The new Mercedes had a direct impact on Karl's company. The following year it produced just over 200 new cars. And Daimler was only part of Karl's competition. By the early 1900s, car companies seemed to be sprouting up everywhere. This was especially evident in the United States, where Ransom Olds's car company produced the first U.S. factory-produced car in 1901 when his Oldsmobile was manufactured. Five years earlier, Henry Ford had developed his quadricycle, a two-cylinder, four-horsepower car. By 1908, he was running a company that would produce 15 million "Model T" cars within a few years while pioneering the use of the assembly line.

Meanwhile at Karl Benz's company, the arguments grew fierce. He didn't want his cars to race. He didn't want them to have engines in the front. He also didn't see the future.[2]

In 1903, he retired from the company that bore his name. He left the business decisions to the friends he'd hired. Six years later, his company designed the fastest car on the planet. The Blitzen Benz had an engine that produced 200 horsepower and would eventually reach speeds of more than 140 miles per hour. When the Blitzen began winning races, the Benz company began getting even more orders.

A painting by Walter Gotschke depicting the Mercedes-Benz W196 in a 1955 automobile race.

Unfortunately, the company soon faced even greater challenges. The Great War (later called World War I) began when the Archduke Ferdinand, the heir to the throne of the Austria-Hungarian Empire, was assassinated in Sarajevo, Serbia, on June 28, 1914. It immediately set in motion a series of events that eventually cost millions of lives. Austria suspected that the assassin's support came from Serbia. In response to the murder, Austria made demands from Serbia. The response was hostile. Austria declared war.

Karl's home country of Germany was a close ally of Austria. So when Austria declared war, Germany became involved as well. Russia supported Serbia. By the fall of 1914, many regions of Europe were battlefields. Before the war's conclusion most of the countries in Europe, along with Canada and the United States, were involved.

It would be called the war to end all wars. The horrors of World War I were so extreme that those who experienced the conflict prayed it would never be repeated. When Germany signed the Armistice (peace treaty) on November 11, 1918, Europe was a vastly different continent. Germany itself was devastated by World War I. Nearly two million of its young men died in the war. By contrast, the United States, which became involved near the conclusion of the war, lost 50,000 soldiers. All told, more than fifteen million people—both soldiers and civilians—died during World War I.

By agreeing to end the war, Germany also agreed to a number of harsh conditions. These included repayments that would cripple the country financially. Businesses struggled. Both the Benz and Daimler companies nearly went broke. In 1924, the two firms agreed to merge, or form one company. It would become famous as Daimler-Benz, and its most prestigious product was the Mercedes-Benz.

The next year Karl was the guest of honor at the Munich Auto Jubilee Parade. He and Bertha rode in their original "Patent-Motorwagen-Benz" at the head of hundreds of vehicles. Spectators gave them a thundering ovation. It was a very different reception from the laughter and ridicule that the car had generated four decades earlier.

Four years later, Karl received more recognition. The Rheinischer Automobil Klub (Rhine Automobile Club) sponsored an "honor run" to honor his achievements. It was almost too late. Karl was critically ill and probably didn't hear the almost continuous sound of cars driving past his home. Many of them had been driven long distances for this special occasion.

Karl Benz died on April 4, 1929. He had lived long enough to see automobiles embraced by millions of people, changing the lives of people around the world. Today if all 350 million cars on the planet were placed bumper to bumper on a six-lane highway, the road would have to stretch 200,000 miles—eight times around the world—to hold them all.

Just over fifty years ago, Germany and the United States were at war with each other. Yet it only took a twenty-minute meeting over coffee in Detroit, Michigan, to combine two of their largest companies. In January, 1998, Germany's Daimler-Benz and United State's Chrysler agreed to merge.

When companies merge—combining their operations to form a single corporation—they do so in part to save money. Instead of ten factories building cars, perhaps they'd only need two or three. Maybe separate accounting or engineering departments could be combined. Sometimes two different models can share some of the same parts. But attempting to put together two companies from different countries and different languages is much more challenging than the usual merger.

The two companies were very different. In general, Chrysler employees were more free-spirited, while Daimler-Benz's people were more rigid. The heads of the two companies argued over many issues. They even disagreed about the size of the new firm's business cards. European cards are larger than the ones commonly used in the United States. The German company won this disagreement.

Despite all the difficulties, the merger went through. Combining Chrysler with Daimler-Benz was the biggest corporate merger in history. The two would be worth over fifty billion dollars. Today the company produces more than four million passenger cars that range in price from $12,000 for a Neon up to $134,000 for a Mercedes-Benz S600. It also produces half a million commercial vehicles such as trucks and buses. More than 350,000 people work for the company.

"We're one company now and we're making it work,"[2] Chrysler president Tom Stallkamp told Time magazine.

In one notable compromise, Daimler-Benz agreed to drop the Benz from its name. The company Karl Benz started is now known as DaimlerChrysler.

# Chronology

| | |
|---|---|
| **1844** | Is born on November 25 in Karlsruhe, Germany |
| **1850s** | Attends Karlsruhe Grammar School |
| **1860** | Attends Karlsruhe's Polytechnic |
| **1864** | Graduates from the Polytechnic |
| **1864-1870** | Works for over half a dozen companies, including an engine manufacturer and a locksmith |
| **1872** | Along with partner August Ritter, opens the "Iron Foundry and Machine Shop"; marries Bertha Ringer |
| **1878** | Begins development of two-stroke engine |
| **1883** | Develops electric ignition system |
| **1885** | Tests "Patent-Motorwagen-Benz," a three-wheeled car with a four-stroke engine |
| **1886** | Demonstrates car in Mannheim |
| **1888** | Bertha drives the car on a 65-mile journey |
| **1893** | Begins production of the first four-wheeled Benz car, the Victoria |
| **1894** | Begins production of first compact car, the Velo |
| **1903** | Steps down from the company |
| **1909** | Blitzen Benz car sets world speed record of 125 miles per hour |
| **1925** | Makes final public appearance in a parade in Munich |
| **1929** | Dies on April 4 |

# Timeline of Discovery

| | |
|---|---|
| **1680** | Christian Huygens, a Dutch physicist and inventor, designs but doesn't construct an internal combustion engine meant to be fueled by gunpowder. |
| **1798** | Muskets with interchangeable parts developed by Eli Whitney are the first "mass-produced" products in the United States. |
| **1807** | Swiss inventor François Isaac de Rivaz creates an internal combustion engine using an oxygen and hydrogen mixture for fuel. The engine doesn't work very well; neither does the "car" he builds for the engine. |
| **1815** | In England, Scottish surveyor John McAdam's method of paving (called macadam) greatly improves road conditions. |
| **1824** | Samuel Brown, an English engineer, rigs an old steam engine to burn gas and uses it to drive a vehicle up London's Shooter's Hill. |
| **1839** | After dropping a mixture of rubber, sulfur and lead on a hot stove, Philadelphian Charles Goodyear accidentally invents "vulcanized rubber," which will later be widely used in tires. |
| **1851** | Independently of each other, Kentucky resident William Kelly and British inventor Sir Henry Bessemer discover a method of blowing air through molten iron to create steel. This metal, which is both stronger than iron and more flexible, will be widely used in automobile manufacturing. |
| **1858** | Jean Joseph Etienne Lenoir of Belgium invents a double-acting, spark ignition internal combustion engine run by coal gas. |
| **1862** | French Civil engineer Alphonse Beau de Rochas patents but never constructs a four-stroke engine. |

43

# Timeline of Discovery (cont'd)

| | |
|---|---|
| **1864** | Austrian Siegfried Marcus attaches a one-cylinder engine he builds to a cart to create the world's first gasoline-powered vehicle. |
| **1876** | Nicolaus August Otto invents the four-stroke motor, a working internal combustion engine that is both safer and more effective than steam engines. |
| **1885** | German Karl Benz builds the first automobile to utilize the internal combustion engine. The next year, fellow German Gottlieb Daimler develops the first motorcycle. |
| **1896** | Henry Ford develops his first car, the quadricycle. |
| **1913** | Henry Ford introduces the moving automobile assembly at his Highland Park plant. |
| **1924** | The firms of Daimler and Benz sign an "agreement of mutual interest" and merge their operations two years later to form Daimler-Benz. |
| **1936** | The first Volkswagen car is produced. |
| **1949** | Mercedes introduces its 170S and 170D, the first new post-war car model designs. |
| **1960** | The state of California introduces the first laws regulating automotive emissions. |
| **1974** | Air bags are introduced to improve safety. |
| **1984** | New York becomes the first state to require people to wear seatbelts while in an automobile. |
| **1997** | Mercedes introduces its first SUV, the ML320. |
| **1998** | Chrysler and Daimler-Benz merge to form DaimlerChrysler. |
| **2000** | DaimlerChrysler acquires controlling interest in Mitsubishi Motors, making the Daimler-Chrysler-Mitsubishi car grouping the world's third largest after General Motors and Ford. |
| **2003** | DaimlerChrysler announces plans to build Mercedes-Benz vans in China. |
| **2004** | The Mercedes-Benz SLK-Class is the trendsetter and technological leader in sports cars. |

# Chapter Notes

**Chapter 2    Sailing with Karl**

1. Beverly Rae Kimnes. *The Star and the Laurel*. (Montvale, N.J.: Mercedes Benz, 1986), p.22.

2. Jason Stein, "Karl Benz", <u>Wheelbase Communications</u>, March 7, 2003.

**Chapter 3    Engine-ering**

1. Robert W Nitske, *Mercedes-Benz: A History*. (Osceola, Wisconsin: Motorbooks International, 1978), p. 22.

2. Ibid., p. 22.

**Chapter 4    Bertha's Caper**

1. Beverly Rae Kimes. *The Star and the Laurel*. (Montvale, N.J.: Mercedes-Benz, 1986), p. 42.

2. Ibid.

3. Jonathan Mantle, *Car Wars*, (New York: Little Brown and Company, 1995), p. 3.

**Chapter 5    Race Cars**

1. 100 years of Mercedes, http://www.geocities.com/ mb420secmercedes100.html

2. Beverly Rae Kimes. *The Star and the Laurel*. (Montvale, N.J.: Mercedes-Benz, 1986), p. 92.

3. Frank Gibney, "Worldwide Fender Blender." *Time* magazine, May 24, 1999.

# Glossary

**assembly line**      method in which workers assemble parts in a certain order

**automation**      assembly of products using machines

**conveyor belt**      thick belt which automatically moves items to workers

**crankshaft**      shaft linked to the rod on the end of the piston that supplies motive power to a vehicle

**cylinder**      tube-like chamber in which a piston moves up and down

**interchangeable**      parts items produced identically so they can be used the same way

**internal combustion engine**      engine in which power is generated by the burning of fuel inside it

**patent**      government document that keeps an invention from being sold or manufactured without inventor's permission for a certain number of years

**piston**      solid metal part that fits inside a cylinder and moves up and down to supply power to a crankshaft

# Further Reading

**For Young Adults**

Corrick, James A. *The Industrial Revolution*. San Diego, California: Lucent Books, Inc., 1998.

Flynn, Mike. *Inside a Car*. Danbury, Connecticut: Grolier Educational, 2001.

*Land and Water Transportation*. Danbury, Connecticut: Grolier Educational, 2000.

*Visual Dictionary of Cars*. New York: Dorling Kindersley Pub, 1992.

Williams, Brian. *Karl Benz*. New York: The Bookwright Press, 1991.

**Works Consulted**

Adler, Dennis. *Mercedes-Benz 110 Years of Excellence*. Osceola, Wisconsin: Motorbooks International, 1995.

Crabb, Richard. *Birth of a Giant*. New York: Chilton Book Company, 1969.

Gibney, Frank. "Worldwide Fender Blender." *Time* magazine, May 24, 1999.

Karwatka, Dennis. "Technology's Past." *Tech Directions*, January, 1997.

Kimes, Beverly Rae. *The Star and the Laurel*. Montvale, N.J.: Mercedes-Benz, 1986.

Mantle, Jonathan. *Car Wars*. New York: Little Brown and Company, 1995.

Nitske, W. Robert. *Mercedes-Benz: A History*. Osceola, Wisconsin: Motorbooks International, 1978.

Schildberger, Freidrich. *Mercedes-Benz: Gottlieb Daimler, Wilhelm Maybach, and Karl Benz*. Stuttgart, Germany: Daimler-Benz, 1968.

Setright, L.J.K. *Mercedes Benz SL & SLC*. Oxford, United Kingdom: Osprey Publishing Limited, 1999.

Stein, Jason. "Karl Benz." *Wheelbase Communications*, March 7, 2003.

**On the Internet**

European Automotive Hall of Fame
www.autonews.com/files/euroauto/inductees/benz.htm

DaimlerChrysler - News
www.daimlerchrysler.com/dccom

Trivia-Car History-Early Cars
www.cybersteering.com/trimain/history/ecars.html

Mercedes-Benz - Museum
www.mercedes-benz.com/com/e/home/heritage/museum/index.html

Mercedes-Benz
www.mercedes-benz.com

Mercedes-Benz for Kids
www.mercedes-benz.com/d/about/kids/index.html

100 years of Mercedes
www.geocities.com/mb420sec/mercedes100.html

Bicycle History
www.pedalinghistory.com/PHbikbio.htm

Cugnot
www.3wheelers.com/cugnot.html

# Index